Copyright © 2018 by Paul Begadon.

All rights are illusory but will be asserted by the Law of Claw and Fang.

*This book or any portion thereof
may not be reproduced or used in any manner without the written permission of the publisher
except for the use of brief quotations.*

Product of the island of Ireland.

Déanta in Éirinn.

First Edition Printing, 2018.

*ISBN-13: 978-1986582025
ISBN-10: 1986582027*

Cover design by Leonardo Albiero.

www.woodkern.net

contact@woodkern.net

What Are You Selling?

By Paul Begadon.

Introduction

Since 2016 I have written, designed, published, and sold my own creations online and in physical form. Between that time and the time of writing these words I have come across countless creative peoples who post pictures and samples of their work online for the entire world to see, and many of these people are producing truly great work. I have seen (and sometimes commissioned) the works of great tattoo artists, animators, painters, printers, writers, designers, craftsmen, and many others.

One thing I have noticed while trawling through the vast body of art that these people are creating is that few of them ever manage to actually barter their work for cold currency. I thought about this for a long time; why is it that so many of these potentially great artists and creators do not earn a living, however meagre it may be, from doing what they are clearly so passionate about?

Despite its limitations, the internet has granted us the ability to create, promote, sell, and profit from the works of our hand and mind with an ease that has never before been available. If you have access to the internet, you really have very few excuses to justify your lack of success as a creator of content or art. This leads me to conclude that the process behind learning how to leverage the power of the internet to their advantage either intimidates many people, or else they are hesitant to embrace the process of selling and the art of salesmanship.

I can testify to this first-hand, as I too have struggled to produce, promote, and sell my original works in exactly the same manner. When I began publishing my writing online on the Unchaining The Titan website, I had no idea how to promote what I was writing and even less of an idea about how to profit from it. My articles were sporadic and varied, often receiving praise and interaction from an international audience, but always my work was published *free gratis*, at no cost. This was because I was writing a blog and was making the same mistake that many bloggers do: writing only as a hobby. At some point during the course of my writing/blogging I decided that I had produced almost enough content to fill a book. The next step was logical, so I wrote some thus far unpublished exclusive content, put a book together, edited it, commissioned artwork, and released the book myself.

Now people were paying me for the work I was doing, despite the fact that most of the content in the published product was freely available on my website already. The exclusive content made up less than twenty percent of the book. This didn't seem to stop people from handing over their hard-earned cash for my product, which only served to encourage me further. However, while that book did sell more than I had anticipated, it failed to live up to its full potential for two reasons: I didn't know what I was doing in terms of publishing, and I completely failed to promote the book.

With the exception of the artwork, I built "Unchaining The Titan: Collected Essays" from the ground up without any previous knowledge of publishing printed literature. This meant the first edition of that work looked like the work of an amateur, a failing that I corrected with the completely overhauled second edition, which looks and reads like the work of a professional.

My second failing was more serious and inexcusable. In the same way that I didn't know anything about publishing a book, I knew nothing about promoting a book either. The first error I remedied using self-education and experimentation, but the second error went unaddressed for quite some time. The reason for my lack of effective content promotion is the same excuse you will hear so many other artists repeat: the process of marketing and salesmanship is difficult and often unsavory.

At least, this was what I continued to tell myself until I grew up and realized a simple universal truth:

We are all selling something.

All of us, no matter what road of life we walk upon, has something that we can contribute to the world which will add value to human existence. I eventually came to realize that every single one of us has a skill, idea, process, philosophy, opinion, insight, or service, which we would like to propagate amongst our peers. Each of us is selling something, even though we may not realize it. I was slow to accept this simple fact, and it took a career change to open my eyes to the truth.

It was about the same period as I published my first book that my time as a soldier ended after nine years, and I moved into the engineering business. Now I found myself on various building sites around Ireland selling and installing heating, ventilation, and energy equipment to customers from both the public and private sectors. I had gone from being a humble soldier and mechanic, doing what I was told and repairing the various machinery that rolled my way, to being an engineer and a salesman. The experience in promotion, sales, and customer relations I was to undertake in this new trade proved to be invaluable to me and has granted me valuable insight into the nature of business and the process of selling your product, whatever it may be.

It took me some time, however, before I learned to put the business lessons I was learning into practice with my own writing. A work colleague of mine once revealed that he had come across my author's website by accident, read a couple of articles, and really enjoyed what he saw. However, he was still somewhat at a loss to understand the unifying theme behind my work. He said it was:

"Interesting and unique, but I don't see what you're trying to sell?"

A fair question, which it got me to thinking. What am I selling? Now, literally speaking, I was selling books and t-shirts, but that's not what he was asking me and that's not what I was really trying to sell. What he was asking me was:

"What's the unifying message, the higher purpose, the grand vision that you're pushing, and why do you bother to push it?"

This is a question which everyone must ask of themselves if they hope to persuade another human being to buy into their work, art, or way of thinking. This simple question led me to begin seriously reconsidering how I approached my writing and the promotion of my writing. The joy of the writer lies in the process of writing, but not all writers relish the work required to sell their writing. This is why so many authors seek out agents and managers and publishers rather than selling their own work. The same can be said of creators of any kind. The creative mind finds its joy in the act of creation, so many lose interest once they have created something and choose to simply move on to the next act of creative expression, lamenting their lack of success or the market's lack of interest in their work.

But it doesn't have to be this way.

In this short (I prefer Laconic) book I will share some of the many lessons I have learned from my experience as a creator, author, and publisher of my own written and graphic compositions, and also from the insights I've gained working in the world of business.

Now, let us be clear on one key point here: it really does not matter what you're selling, or what industry you're in, because the concepts that I will here discuss will be as close to universal as it is possible for me to fathom. So, for example, you know that I sell my own written and graphic work online. But in my "day job" as an Engineer I sell and install energy technology to the commercial and residential sectors. So, whether I'm selling you a Heat Pump to keep your house warm, or my latest book to keep your spirit warm, the essence of the process will be the same in both cases.

It is the theory and practice of selling whatever you sell that we will here discuss, and that information will be relevant in any field or industry.

However, let it be made clear right here at the beginning of our journey, that those who stand to gain the most from this work will be the creators, like myself and many among my audience, who wish to know more about promoting and distributing their own creations. I have seen so many people producing great work online that never sees the light of day because their promotional efforts cease at a limp Facebook post saying some half-hearted, weak drivel like *"Check out my new handmade skinny jeans..."* or *"Here's my latest painting of the Patriarchy. Buy it now for only ten male scalps".* Weak, uninteresting noise the likes of which I too was putting out before I got serious.

If this sounds like you do when promoting your own stuff, then ask yourself the following:

Ask yourself, who in their right mind would buy something from you when your marketing strategy (or lack thereof) demonstrates that you clearly don't give a shit?

And while you're at it, ask yourself a series of other questions which will give you the answers you need to become exponentially more effective in distributing your work, or those works which you sell on behalf of others. It is this series of questions which we will explore throughout the rest of this book, and we will begin with the most basic and obvious...

What Are You Selling?

Firstly, we must understand that every single one of us is selling something, even if we aren't pushing it very hard or charging any money to access it. Unless we are completely spineless, irrelevant sponge-bones, then we probably have some sort of opinion, agenda, or ambition that we would like to make manifest in the physical realm. We say we have "dreams" or "ambitions", but this alone is merely an act of visualization or a fantasy. Visualization is important, in fact it's essential, but it means nothing if we do not take purposeful, directed action to make our dreams and ambitions manifested in our lives. Often this means that we must recruit others where they might align with and assist our mission. To recruit others, we must convince them to align with our way of thinking, and in order to convince them we must sell them something. The creator and the artist and the craftsman in particular must become familiar with the nuances of salesmanship or his work will go forever unnoticed among the crowd of other distractions crying out for our attention on a daily basis.

Salesmanship can be a dirty word in some people's minds because of the many negative connotations associated with it. When we think of a "Salesman", we think of someone who is greasy, deceptive, profit-driven, vacuous, and dishonorable. Salesmen are those annoying pests who talk too much, listen too little, lie with intent, take your money, and then vanish into thin air cackling like witches, right?

Let's get real here and admit that's childish nonsense. To "sell" something is to convince another person that that thing has value, and that its value is sufficient to justify them making a financial sacrifice to obtain it. If I create something, be it a book or a painting or a musical recording or a piece of furniture, which I believe to have value, then I'd better learn to convince you that is has value too. I'd better learn to sell it. Too many great artists go unappreciated because they focus all of their creative energies on the process of creation itself, which is where the artist's joy is to be found, but they neglect to creatively focus on the art of selling their creations, which can often be tedious and unsatisfying work.

When I use the word "sell", what I mean is "to push or promote our ideas or our will onto a third party". I can "sell" you something without charging you a penny, but I am still playing the part of the salesman so long as I am trying to convince you to see things my way. If I'm offering you free advice on your mortgage, it's because I'm promoting whatever financial methodology I'm sharing with you. If I join Greenpeace and assault whaling vessels in the Pacific Ocean, then upload videos or do interviews about it, I'm selling the idea that whales must be protected by any means necessary. If I record a video of myself performing a song of my own and upload it to YouTube, I'm selling my music or the message behind my music. If I record an album and do a radio interview discussing it, then I'm selling the album and also my music as a whole. As for me, I write books and I design t-shirts. These are the products that I sell, books and apparel, but what I'm actually selling is the body of ideas that unify my worldview and sum up to the total of my Brand Identity. I'm selling ideas in the form of physical product. When you really think about it, what I'm selling is the nothing that was once my own thought but which has been manifested in physical form. That is essentially what all art is and it is this physical form that we must learn to sell if we want our art to be noticed, evaluated, shared, and profitable.

All businesses must know exactly who they are and what they sell. The penalty for confusion or ambiguity concerning your brand's identity and soul is iniquity, anonymity, failure, and death. Many good businesses in the hands of competent operators have fallen into ruin for committing the unforgiveable sin of not truly understanding what they sell.

Example:
Borders was a major player in the printed book market for decades, operating out of multiple stores from 1971 to 2011. The sun finally set on the Borders empire after they were taken over by Kmart, who had struggled for years to make their own bookstore brand, Waldenbooks, successful. Kmart hoped that the experienced senior management of Borders would be able to do what Waldenbooks management had failed to do for so long. However, many of the key management figures in Borders simply quit rather than merge with a lesser brand. Devoid of its most experienced leadership figures, Borders began over-investing in unfamiliar products like CDs and DVDs, even selling toys and clothing. For a long time Borders was seen as a business that was owned, managed, staffed, and frequented by book lovers, dedicated enthusiasts of the printed word. Borders' identity was all about the experience of searching out and buying books but had nothing to do with music, toys, and DVDs. Borders wasn't just selling books to its customers, it was selling the Borders experience. You could walk into the store without a clue what you were looking for, just a vague notion of what you might like to read about, and the genuinely friendly staff there would know what books to steer you towards, where those books were located, and how many were in stock. The staff loved their jobs and this enthusiasm was infectiously apparent to those customers they interacted with, but over time this love began to die out. Customer testimonials state that a major

reason they abandoned Borders in favor of its competitors was that they lost the joy of the Borders experience. They could still get the same books at the same prices, but the staff/customer/brand interaction became stale and lifeless. Why shop at Borders when you could get the same product and experience elsewhere, often at a lower cost? Of course, I am here focusing only on one of a number of reasons that led to the dissolution of the Borders brand, though it is no exaggeration to say that a major contributor to the death of this once beloved brand was that it lost sight of what it was selling. The company thought it was selling books but forgot that it was actually selling a book buying experience, which brought happiness to the book lovers who walked into the store. The CDs, the DVDs, the toys, the soulless modernized store design, the loss of brand personality, all paved the road to ruin upon which this once mighty business rolled into its grave.

So now we should have an appreciation of the relevance of the salesman's craft and the importance of knowing exactly what you have to offer to prospective clients. But to be successful in promoting our art or business we must follow a proven process and anticipate the many questions which we must be prepared to answer when we try to convince others of our art's intrinsic value. In this work I will examine some of the most common questions we will be asked, either verbally or inverbally, when we try to sell whatever we sell. It is imperative that you ask yourself these same questions and become proficient in convincing people through the clarity and authentic enthusiasm of your answers. The first question you must ask (*"What am I selling?"*) has already been sufficiently discussed. The next question that naturally arises is:

Why Do I Sell What I'm Selling?

The answer to this should be obvious, right?

For the big bag of cash!

Well, that's part of the reason, but a big payoff is never guaranteed and that alone is rarely sufficient motivation. A more typical (and far more desirable) motivation would be:

"I'm selling it because I believe in it and because I believe it provides value."

But you can believe in something and keep it to yourself, right? Sure, but if you have gone to the effort of creating something then it's probably something that you consider valuable, and unless you're totally unlike the rest of mankind, the chances are it will provide value for someone else too.

It's my opinion that what I sell has the potential to benefit and improve the quality of life of others in the same way that it improves the quality of my life on a daily basis. So I sell what I sell because I believe that it is valuable, I believe that I am good at it, and I want to share what interests and inspires me with others of like mind. Using my first book "Unchaining The

Titan" as an example, it contains mythological and historically validated wisdom which has survived many centuries of time because the information contained therein is worth something, otherwise it would have been forgotten. I find value in its contents and so I try to convince people that they too can find value in it. You must learn to find and explain, in detail, the value and worthiness of your own creation before you can ever expect anyone else to make a financial sacrifice to obtain it.

Knowing your reason "Why?" is one of the key steps towards establishing your Brand Identity, which will decide how you interact with your chosen Niche. Your reason for selling must align with your niche's reason for buying, and it is your job to create a well-trod path between your buyer's identity and your brand's identity.

Brand Identity is a vital concept to understand, and it is one of the most important aspects of your business to develop and carefully maintain. It is composed of a number of key components, each of which bears further explanation. I find it useful to sketch Brand Identity graphs so I can put down everything relevant about the Brand on a single page. The Identity graph should look something like this:

APPEARANCE	PROVIDER	CHARACTER
RELATIONSHIP	**YOUR BRAND**	CULTURE
NICHE	BENEFICIARY	SELF-IMAGE

This graphic sketch of your Brand Identity briefly plots the following:

Provider – Who is the creator/operator of the brand? Who does the customer see at the helm? Is it you or someone more relatable? Does the Provider figure truly embody the spirit of the Brand? If not, what can you do to make the Provider more relatable to your audience? Consider Richard Branson, founder of the Virgin Group, who actively represents the many subsets of his group in the public eye.

Beneficiary – Who will benefit from your brand's offer? This is not the same as your Niche, but rather it is a subset of your Niche. Who among your chosen market will really gain the most benefit from owning your product or utilizing your service? For many, your brand will be only a passing interest. But for the true Beneficiary, your brand will become a part of their life.

Appearance – What kind of recurring visual symbols/colours/themes will the brand use in its graphics? What is your logo and what does it evoke? Why do you use specific colours? What symbols may be associated with your brand in a congruent manner? For example, the symbols of the Shield and the Eagle are associated with Harley Davidson motorcycles. The Eagle suggests freedom and flight, whereas the Shield suggest strength, security, and individualism. What are your Brand's symbols and how do they relate to your offer?

Relationship – How does the customer interact with the brand and vice versa? Social Media is great, but it is only one level on the ladder of interaction. Are there groups for your customers only? Do you meet them face to face? What benefits do returning customers gain by their loyalty? Do you do Q&A sessions? Do you take suggestions and embrace feedback, or simply do your own thing? Are you accountable to your audience or do you hide away from them? Different brands will benefit from differing levels of interaction, so figure out how much you should interact and what the most effective form of interaction will be.

Niche – What group of people does the brand actively target? People are diverse in character and you have no hope of appealing to everyone equally, nor should you wish to. Do your research and determine what general group of people share interests or problems which relate to your Brand or Offer. What do they have in common? What goals do they aspire to and what obstacles stand in their path? How can you help them to succeed in whatever struggles and challenges they face?

Character – What person or archetype most embodies the Brand Identity? Is there a celebrity who could represent your work and can you get them involved somehow? Maybe you should craft an identity or a character to use as your brand mascot, just like the rugged Marlboro Man or the humorous Mr. Muscle. Maybe you yourself might serve as a suitable representative for your brand, just like the image of Colonel Saunders does for KFC.

Culture – What do those who align with the Brand Identity do in order to belong to that Identity? What are their rituals? Do they ride motorcycles? Do they work out? Do they read? Are they artists or entrepreneurs themselves? Your Brand Culture is defined by those activities which qualify someone for inclusion in your Brand Identity. What actions differentiate those inside the group to those on the outside? Focus here on action rather than mere ideas or shared opinions. Deeds will always be superior to words, and you must waste no time in catering to those who relate to your work through lip service alone.

Self-Image – How do the brand's Beneficiaries perceive themselves? Is their sense of self-worth determined by their relationship to the spirit which your Brand embodies or its culture? Does engaging in your Identity's rituals improve their self-esteem or make them feel worse about themselves? You must strive to ensure that those who stand to benefit from your offer always experience positive interactions with your service and your Brand Identity. Let them know that you give a shit and they just might return the favour.

Consider all of these different aspects of your own brand thoroughly, draw them out so you can see them all at once, then use that information to purposefully craft a Brand Identity which will draw in members of your Niche and sustain their loyalty. Often a brand will enjoy brief period of success before its customer's move over to the competition, and many times this is simply because the brand had a weak or non-existent Identity strategy. Do not be one of these brands. Be purposeful and prepared.

Every action, deed, comment, status update, promotional message, image, email, video, and conversation that people see concerning you or your brand must be consistent with a pre-determined Identity which builds upon, and never deviates from, your Mission Statement.

Without a clearly defined Mission Statement for your brand you will operate without focus and without a nucleus around which to build your Brand Identity. A Mission Statement is a brief description of what you sell, who you sell it to, and why it is unique or superior to its competitors. It unites all aspects of your brand around a common objective, towards which you aim and never deviate from. Many aspects of your business will change over time, but your Mission should remain the same. This is why I recommend you spend time developing your Mission Statement until it is razor sharp. Sentences which contain only the bare minimum number of words required to express their message are referred to as Laconic, because of the speech among the citizens of ancient Sparta (Lacedaemon), and you should strive to make your Mission Statement as Laconic as possible. Consider TED's mission: "Spread Ideas".

Not every mission can be reduced to two words, so don't worry if your final statement runs into a few sentences. What matters is that you take time to define your mission as clearly as possible, and allow that mission to serve as the end goal which every action your brand takes moves you progressively closer to reaching. Without a clear and concise Mission Statement you will struggle to build a consistent Brand Identity, which will confuse and frustrate your customer base, driving them into the arms of your competitors. Know what you hope to achieve by doing what you do and selling what you sell.

Example:
Operation Werewolf is a multi-tiered program of total life reform, which promises to improve its customer's lives on the physical, mental, and spiritual planes. The company publishes printed material, instructional videos, eBooks, nutritional guides, strength and conditioning programs, and graphic zines online. It also sells custom apparel and hosts events and workshops in a variety of locations on both sides of the globe. This is an impressive range of products and services to be on offer when you consider that Operation Werewolf is currently spearheaded by one man, with contributions from a few other key individuals. However, despite its versatility, where OPWW truly stands out as an exemplar to other

businesses is in the careful maintenance and development of its Brand Identity. OPWW regularly posts on social media depicting interactions with Operatives from across the world, often in real face-to-face meetings, and the Brand's published content is always consonant with the overarching Identity and Mission. Its social content shows men and women who are physically capable, well read, thoughtful, creative, and interesting, participating in mysterious rituals which are specific to the Brand Identity. Customers of OPWW do not feel like mere customers when interacting with the brand, they feel like members of an in-group, a unique organization with its own language, mythology, rituals, and symbolism. To reinforce this collective Identity, OPWW never refers to its customers as "customers", but rather as "Operatives", thus reinforcing the client's personal identity as an operative within a collective and ongoing Operation. This is no mere marketing trick however, as many "Operatives" do in fact band together and form tribal groups with identities that are consonant with and influenced by Operation Werewolf. To look at it from the outside, it has the appearance of a tribe or a cult more-so than a business, which is exactly what a successful Brand Identity should look like to the uninitiated eye.

Consider the following Brand Identity map for Harley Davidson, which plots many key aspects of the Harley experience.

APPEARANCE	PROVIDER	CHARACTER
Iconic Harley Logo. American Eagle. Signature Harley Style. Range of Merchandise.	American Company. Long Storied History. Iconic Brand.	Outlaw MC Members (The 1%) Peter Fonda (Easy Rider) Lee Marvin (The Wild One) Mickey Rourke
RELATIONSHIP	**YOUR BRAND**	**CULTURE**
Dealers all over the world. Presence at shows/expos. Learn to Ride Programme.		Ride Motorcycles. Customize Motorcycles. Club Members. Harley Owners Group.
NICHE	**BENEFICIARY**	**SELF-IMAGE**
Middle-aged men (35+). Chopper Enthusiasts. Patriotic Riders.	Riders who love freedom, rebellion, choppers, history, America.	Free Spirits. Outlaws. Rebels.

Who Am I Selling To?

You can't please everyone, so don't waste your energy trying to be all things to all Men. Your product, whatever it is, will only be appealing to a certain kind of person, who lives a certain kind of life and has a certain kind of problem. You must research and understand who your offer will apply to most, and tailor your offer so that these people cannot resist the compulsion to invest in your brand. One useful technique for researching your niche is readily available to everyone who is not a psychopath or severely autistic:

Empathy.

To understand your niche, the market subset who will be most receptive to your offer, you must get inside their skin. First, you must determine who you should focus your efforts in selling to. Next, you must build character profiles to describe the different types of person in your niche. Then, you must learn to experience life as they experience it. This is where empathy is key. What problems does your prospect have in their life? If you share those problems, how does it make you feel? How do you deal with them? What ambitions do your prospects have and what obstacles prevent them from making those ambitions manifest? If those obstacles are real, how might they be overcome? If those obstacles are imagined, what mental-shift must occur to remove them?

I find it useful to sketch out an Empathy Map to help me get in my prospect's skin. The Empathy Map is a brief exercise which forces you to think like the receiver of your offer would think, which can be hard to do intuitively without a visual aid. This exercise needn't be overly formalized or structured, a simple sketch will do. It doesn't really matter how well-crafted this Map looks, what really matters is the amount of effort you put into researching its contents. I deliberately sketch my Empathy Maps out quickly, so that I waste no more time than necessary on drawing it. Focus rather on filling it in using as much real-world data as you can get your hands on and researching the Character Profiles within your Niche. It doesn't have to be pretty (mine certainly aren't), but it should look something like this:

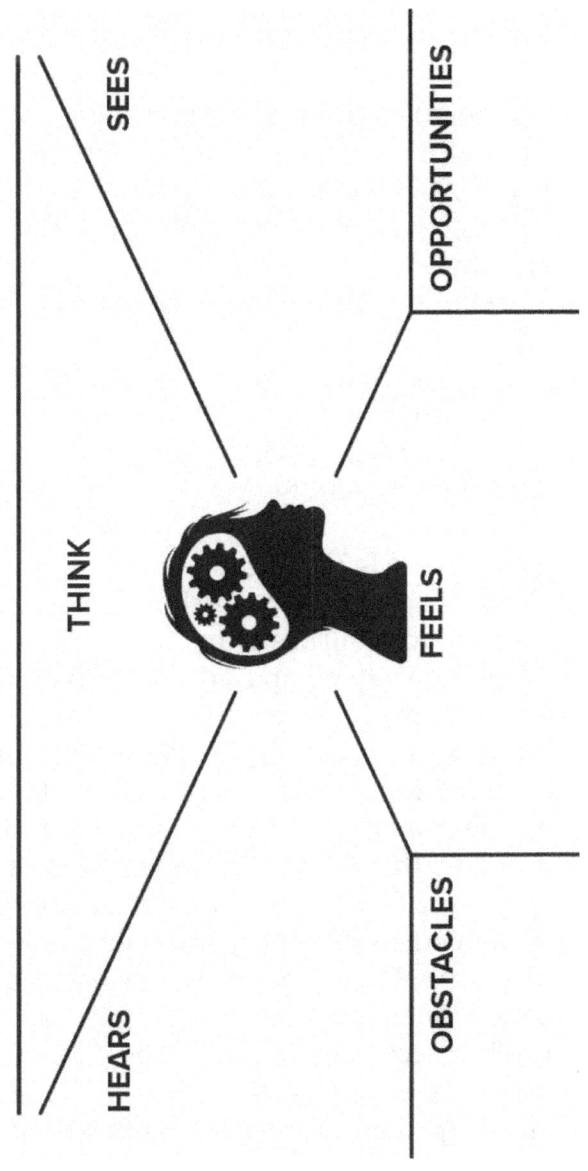

Notice the 7 key sections of the Map: Character, Thoughts, Feelings, Seeing, Hearing, Obstacles, and Opportunities. In order, these describe:

Character - Who your customer is.
Thoughts - What they think about your offer.
Feelings - What emotions your offer triggers.
Seeing - How your offer appears to them visually.
Hearing - What they hear others say about your offer.
Obstacles - Why they may be reluctant to invest in your offer.
Opportunities - What they stand to gain by investing in your offer.

It will be useful to complete several Empathy Maps relating to each of the different Character Profiles you will focus on selling to. After all, a niche is rarely composed of one type of person alone. Sure, if all you're selling is left-handed scissors you will have the good fortune of knowing exactly who you're selling to and what problem they need to overcome, but most of us won't be that lucky. Put the effort in at the very beginning of your product development and get to know the different types of people you should focus on selling to. Segment this list into different bands, then rank your prospective Character Profiles according to those who stand to be most receptive to your offer. In the building of Profiles and Maps and Segments it is essential that you keep it real, and don't get lazy by skipping over the exercise or inventing false data.

Use as much real-world data as possible when creating your Empathy Map. Use research tools such as social networks, surveys, cold calls, testimonials, sample products for review etc. If your social media profile has a number of bad reviews on it, then prospects will see and/or hear these criticisms and their thoughts and emotions will be affected accordingly. Write this information down on your Empathy Map. Likewise, if someone you know might stand to gain from your product, give them a freebie if they will give you honest feedback. If you're reluctant to give away your work for free, give them a free sample with the proviso that if they find it useful they will pay for it, and if they find it useless they will tell you exactly why in detail. Real-world data from actual human beings is far more valuable than sitting at a computer conducting market research from products and niches which may or may not bear any relation to your own. You can know your niche best by interacting with them directly in a professional yet personable manner.

I struggled with this process during the development of my first book, "Unchaining The Titan". That product consists primarily of written works which incorporate a variety of themes and topics that do not often match up in an obvious way. Sometimes I write about history, sometimes about psychology, and often about mythology. On the surface of it my work can look fragmentary and incohesive, so I had to learn to find and explain the commonalities that tie it all together. It's important to know what the overall point of one's body of work is as a whole, so one must look for the commonalities that unite what can often seem disparate and fractured. My writing usually deals with some aspect of mythology, history, or legend, then draws parallels between the topic in question and modern life, before summarizing what I believe the modern reader can stand to gain by learning from the lessons of the topic being discussed. In short, I take what is old, and I try to make it relevant to what is new. This is why Unchaining The Titan's Mission Statement was "Modern Applications of Old Knowledge".

As I'm sure you have noticed, this is a very broad summary of what is essentially a unique niche. Some trends within my own audience that I have noticed are that many of my readers share an interest in European Mythology, History, Legend, Psychology, Spiritualism, Archetypes, Physical Strength, Paganism, Storytelling, Weightlifting, Woodcraft, and Self-Improvement. This has been my audience to date and these are the people that I sell to, because these people are often very much like me. Because we share the same interests we can both have an appreciation of what it is that I am selling. I can get inside their skin because we are of like mind and probably have similar problems. My point is, I would never know or understand the people who are most likely to value my work if I did not take the time to seek them out, both online and in person, and to learn how they think.

This is what I mean when I talk about a niche. Everyone has one. Find yours and speak directly to the people within it, because they are the ones most likely to buy what you are selling. Don't waste time trying to convince people who do not value your offer. Discover the people who do value your offer and strive wholeheartedly to make allies and customers of them. Remember, you should be aiming to provide a valuable solution to a real-world problem, not wasting time and energy (and money) in preaching to those with no ears to hear your sermons.

Example:
TJ Brutal Customs fabricates custom modifications for the Honda Shadow motorcycle, and only the Honda Shadow motorcycle. This is a guy who wanted to customize his own Shadow just like all those Harley owners have been doing for decades but couldn't find the cool parts that he wanted. So, he made them himself. Bear in mind, the custom motorcycle market is huge, but in the USA, it is dominated by Harley Davidson. Which is fine, but what if you don't ride a Harley? The Shadow is a very popular motorcycle with a lot of riders who look at custom Harley Davidsons on a daily basis and want to chop their Hondas too. I ride a custom

Shadow, as do others I know, and I can testify to this fact. TJ Brutal Customs has zoned in on a very specific niche, Honda Shadow owners, and offered them a valuable service which is not readily available elsewhere. He knows exactly what he's selling and who he's selling to.

You might think that TJ Brutal Customs has committed a grave sin in ignoring the deep well of potential customers who want to chop their motorcycles but who don't ride a Honda Shadow. Why not offer custom parts for Harleys too? The problem is, the custom Harley market is saturated with suppliers, and any new supplier to this market would find themselves screaming in a crowd, whereas the custom Honda Shadow market is much less populated, leaving TJ Brutal Customs in a prominent position to grab the attention of his chosen niche. You do not have to offer a unique product that can't be gotten elsewhere to succeed, but it certainly does help.

You must not only know who your niche is, but also where they currently buy what you are offering them, or if they can buy what you are offering them at all. Invest the time in researching your prospective clients thoroughly to the point where you can think and feel like they do when considering your offer. Get inside their skin.

Consider the following sample Empathy Map for one of TJ Brutal Customs' prospects:

PROFILE

John wants to chop his Honda Shadow into a Bobber. He wants quality parts that he can fit himself without special tools or experience.

THINK
"I wish my Shadow was more unique, like a Bobber."

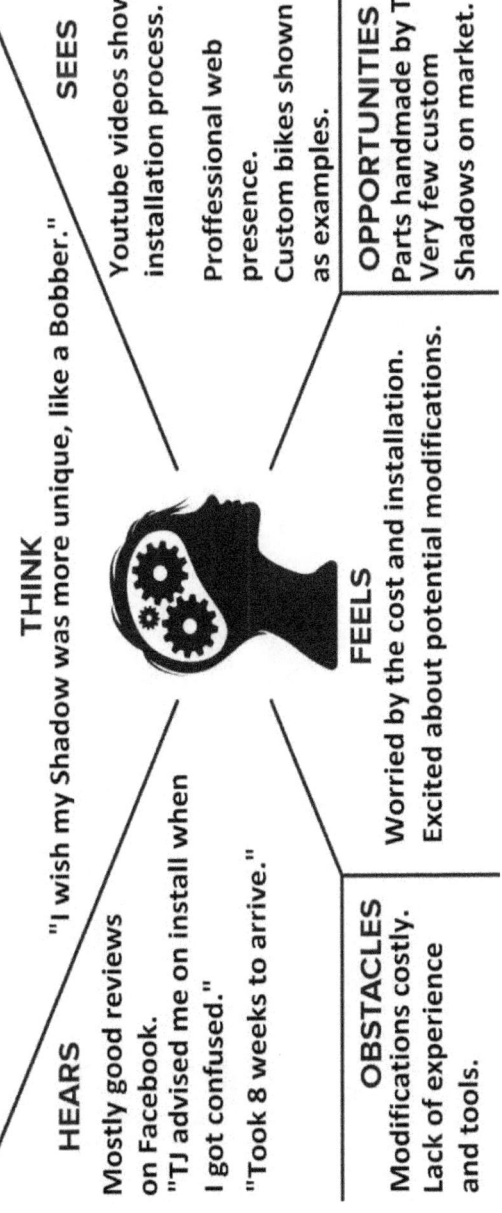

HEARS
Mostly good reviews on Facebook.
"TJ advised me on install when I got confused."
"Took 8 weeks to arrive."

SEES
Youtube videos show installation process.
Proffessional web presence.
Custom bikes shown as examples.

FEELS
Worried by the cost and installation.
Excited about potential modifications.

OBSTACLES
Modifications costly.
Lack of experience and tools.

OPPORTUNITIES
Parts handmade by TJ.
Very few custom Shadows on market.

Why Is What I Sell Better Than Similar Products?

In art, as in business, competition is fierce. Whatever you're doing, whatever you're creating, lots of other people are creating similar things which are just as good as, or better than, yours. It is your job as creator and custodian of your art to ensure that your work stands out from the crowd. These days we are harangued by an unprecedented number of distractions and baubles, which constantly vie for our attention and beg us to commit our time and resources. But each of us has only a finite amount of time, attention, and resources. If you have created something and you want it to succeed, you must learn to compare and contrast it with similar products and find a way to explain why yours is superior. Your tattoos may be good, but many people do great tattoos, so why should I care about yours? Likewise, your book may be a great read but if you can't make it stand out from the thousands of other books that promise me the exact same thing as yours, why should I care?

I will never care about what you are creating until you can present it in such a way that it appeals to me or intrigues me, and you will never care about my work until I do the same. When I tell people that I have published a book the first question they inevitably ask is:

"What's it about?"

At this point I am given a brief opportunity to convince them that my book might be of to benefit that person's life, or at the very least appeal to their interests. From experience, I can tell you this: learn to describe your product's features and benefits in as clear and succinct a statement as possible.

When considering a physical product, features and benefits may seem like the same thing but in fact they are very distinct and very important to comprehend. The features of your product are those aspects which define it as a product, such as its shape, size, colour, texture, material etc. Features are descriptive in nature and do not provide value to your customer. Value is provided only by the benefits. The benefits of your product are the positive effects that possessing the product will have in its owner's life. Some features of the product will be beneficial to a certain type of customer, and your job is to help your customer to understand the benefits which these features will yield.

Remember: nobody cares what your product does, only how what it does will help them.

Consider this book. It is a short work which introduces the basic concepts of salesmanship through the examination of five different questions relating to the reader's potential business offers. Briefly, those are the features of this book. The benefits? Developing relevant answers for the five questions within this book is guaranteed to improve your promotional efforts for whatever product or service that you provide, leading to more prospect interaction and increased sales. I say it is guaranteed without reservation, because the principles I am talking about have been proven by time and are universally applicable to all kinds of business. Taken by themselves, the features of this book are boring, while the benefits are only marginally of interest. The most powerful description of your product will be the one which succinctly presents both the features and the benefits to your prospect, so that they immediately recognize your product's potential to solve their problem.

Now, I have already said that your product must solve a problem for your prospect. If your product actually does solve somebody's problem, then it will be of benefit to them, and you should market your product directly to this group (or niche) of people, but you will have more success if you emphasize your product's benefits more than its features. Present both, but sell the benefits.

Consider the following: you have designed a vehicle which has very low fuel consumption. The main feature of your vehicle is that it has a fuel consumption of x miles per gallon, which is much lower than the norm. Good for you, but this information alone is of no benefit to your prospect. You can convert this feature (low fuel consumption) into a benefit by simply describing how much money your prospect will save by driving your vehicle instead of your competitor's vehicle. But don't make the mistake of boring your prospect during your description, or they will simply write off your offer as uninteresting before you're even finished. Use the insights you gained when you built your Empathy Maps to present your product in a relatable and appealing manner, so that your customer immediately sees the potential benefit of investing in you and in what you are selling.

For example, in one of your Empathy Maps your research may have shown how your prospect is running their own business and seeking to reduce their operating costs. You also know they have a vehicle or vehicles on the road to carry out their work. Quantifying the money they stand to save by replacing their thirsty vehicles with your fuel-efficient vehicle will immediately gain their attention, at which point you can develop your offer more fully.

Do not seek to win over the heart of your prospect with a dull sales pitch that halfheartedly promotes the features of your product and exaggerates its potential benefits. This will trigger your listener's defenses and close their minds off to you. You will be far more successful in promoting your product by placing both your product and your prospective client within the framework of a story. Tell a tale relating your prospect's problems and position your product as the solution to those problems. This approach is semantic and empathetic, which will appeal directly to your listener's emotions and subconscious, rather than their conscious mind. The artist must be a salesman, but the salesman must also be a storyteller.

Whatever your product, you need to make it seem different to its competitors. It must SEEM different, even if it is exactly the same. Find a way to make it unique, or a way to make it seem unique. The thing that differentiates your offer from your competitor's offer is called a USP, a Unique Selling Point, and every salesman must know his USPs inside and out. Don't just say your product is "High Quality" or "User Friendly", because generic terms like these are considered the norm, not anything special. Why would anyone buy a poor quality, difficult to use, piece of crap? When describing your USPs, use your imagination and be specific. What exactly makes your product high quality? Is it manufactured in a specific way or from a certain material? Why exactly is it easier to use than the competition? Does it achieve the same objective but in fewer steps? Differentiate yourself and your brand from all the others who are vying for your niche's attention.

When considering your USP you will inevitably come up with many of the same statements that your competitors will. Do not market your product based on the same USP as the competition. This will force you to compete where you may not need to. Focus on developing a USP which is truly unique to your offer. For example, Domino's pizza guaranteed 30-minute delivery time or less on every order, otherwise it's free. Domino's make cheap pizza, which tastes essentially the same as every other cheap pizzeria out there, but no other pizzeria guaranteed delivery in 30 minutes. People bought Domino's hoping that their delivery would be late just so they would get it free. This guarantee put Domino's in a prominent position in their customer's minds and in the take-out Pizza market.

Consider the following USP diagram for Snap-On tools, who offer a lifetime replacement guarantee on their range of hand tools. I have availed of this tool warranty and will admit that the peace of mind the lifetime guarantee affords was a major factor in my buying Snap-On rather than cheaper alternatives. The tools were likely the same quality as the alternatives, but I felt they were superior because of the peace of mind the guarantee granted.

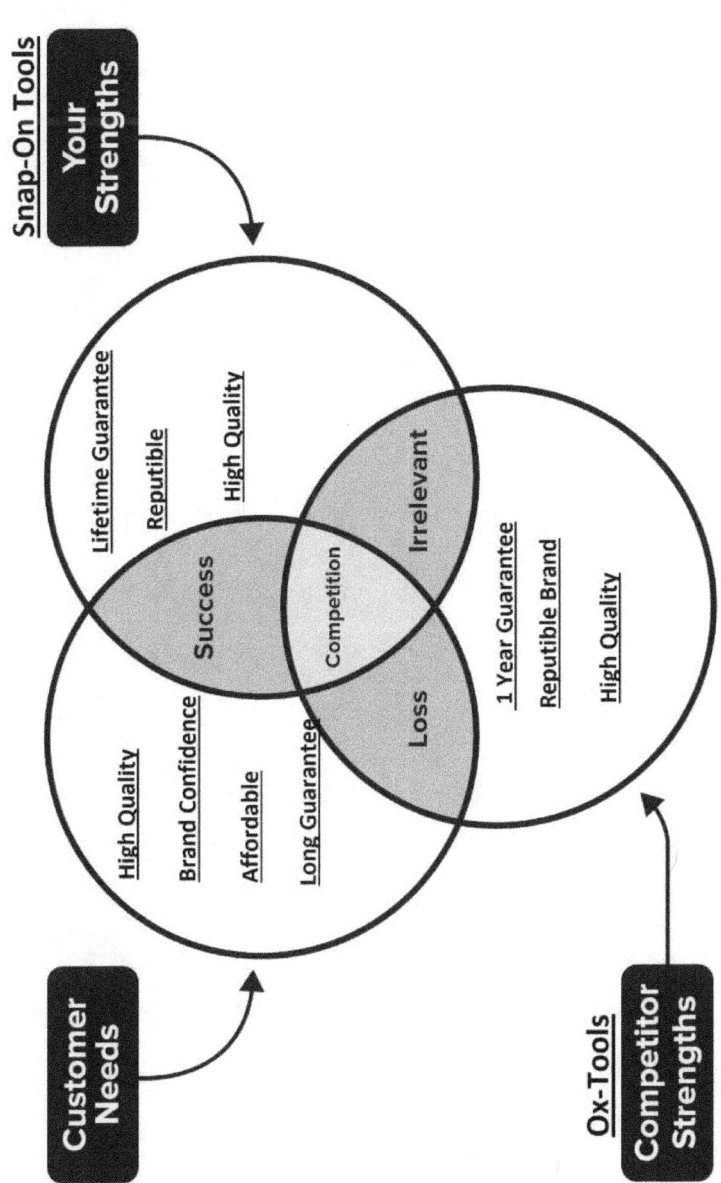

Why Should You Buy What I Sell?

It is perfectly reasonable for someone to ask what they stand to gain by investing time or resources into your particular product. You could be the greatest painter on the planet, but why should I give a shit? Is your painting something that I even want or need? If you are a strength coach, what makes your strength and conditioning program any different from the countless others on the market? These are questions you must anticipate and prepare for, or you will be left at a loss for words when you try to make the sale.

I have already talked about creating value and this is exactly where the value of your work is most relevant. It doesn't really matter what your particular creation is, everything has the potential to make some positive contribution to the world and the people within it. Figure out what the potential of your own creation is and figure out the ways in which it applies to your niche. You may think your work has value and the potential to improve the lives of others, but you need to convince me before you can expect me to buy into it. What does the customer stand to gain by investing in your art? Convince yourself before you even attempt to convince someone else.

If your product is nothing more than a "nice-to-know" or a bauble to be used merely as adornment, then you may well happen to find success, but it will be difficult. People are not stupid, though they are persuadable, and they know instinctively when something has value and when it does not. Your prospects will view your product and immediately decide if what you're offering will solve a problem or improve the quality of their lives. I could probably convince somebody out there to invest in a range of avant-garde designer trashcans, but it would be a damned hard sell. Why? Because a trashcan has a function, and there is very little one could do to improve on this function without rendering the trashcan overly expensive or complex. My product would be attempting to solve a problem that doesn't exist. Unless your product offers a viable solution to make your prospect's lives measurably better or less arduous, they will not see it as having any value.

This is essential, so do not skim over this concept: Your product, service, or idea, must solve a problem for your potential customer which they cannot more appropriately solve by other means. Ask yourself if your work has a function. Research which other products serve the same function, and who is buying them. This is your Niche. Research what problems those in your niche must overcome on a regular basis. Tailor your product in such a way that it not only solves these problems as well as your competitors do, but also try to make your product the most attractive option for the members of your niche.

One minor deviation from the norm when it comes to product benefits are those products which serve primarily as a means of Identity Signaling. Some customers only buy a certain product because it serves a signal to others that they belong to a certain group or tribe, or that they embody a certain ideal. This is why many people buy Harleys, football jerseys, flags, banners, promotional apparel, and those stupid looking rubber wristbands. They only care about that product because of what it symbolically represents, not what tangible benefits it can provide. Sure, a t-shirt with "ABORTIONS FOR ALL" written on it will provide all the benefits of a t-shirt which says "NIKE", but the person wearing the "ABORTIONS FOR ALL" shirt is probably only doing so because of the blatant message scrawled across it for the world to see.

If your product serves only as an Identity Signal, that's not a problem, but make sure you market it as that to the people who align themselves with the same identity. Don't pretend your t-shirt will save the world.

In Conclusion

What are you selling?
Why are you selling it?
Who are you selling to?
Why is it better than the competition?
Why should I buy it?

These are all common questions that any businessman worth his salt will understand, but which can often be overlooked by other less conventional salesmen such as writers, artists, musicians, tattoo artists, public speakers, vloggers, craftsmen, and small-business owners.

Maybe you are a school student wondering what to do with their life, or an entrepreneur, or an artist, or a musician, or maybe you're just trying to make a little extra on the side. Regardless of what field you work in, if you are creative in any way and you want your creations to be noticed, evaluated, and appreciated, then you'd better learn to sell your goods or services or ideas.

Maybe you sell artwork, or music, or your services as a personal trainer, or custom furniture, or handmade knives. Whatever it is that you're selling, ask yourself the questions discussed above and write down some well thought out answers to those questions, because when you try to sell me whatever it is that you're selling, I'll be asking those same questions of your work. Your job is to sell me that work before I have the chance to reason my way out of buying it, or before I lose interest completely.

We are all talented in some way or other, and the internet has afforded unprecedented power to the individual who is willing to act on the opportunities it provides. However, talent and creative ability are worthless if we cannot convince others to value our work. The art of creating value is the art of salesmanship, and the artist who cannot sell his art, like the philosopher who cannot sell his philosophy, or the General who cannot sell his war, is doomed to be forgotten.

What are you selling and why should I care?

Debriefing

Thank you for reading this work.

I have been creating and selling my work and the work of others both professionally and personally for some years now, and gained many important insights into the selling process along the way.

However, when I sat down to write this work, I was forced to consider, evaluate, and refine everything I thought I knew about this topic. Ideas that did not survive this refinement process were discarded, whilst other ideas were solidified and more fully developed.

This process of retrospective thought and writing has served as a valuable education for me, and I truly hope it will serve you just as well.

If you are putting the information found herein to good use in your own life or business, seek me out and let me know what you are doing.

I can be contacted online at my author's website, as well as on the usual social media platforms.

Tell me what you're selling, and maybe I'll buy into it.

www.ingramcontent.com/pod-product-compliance
Lightning Source LLC
Chambersburg PA
CBHW070417230526
45471CB00006B/2854